ACA Common Core Critical Thinking Teacher's Manual
Grades 2 - 4

for

Aesop's Childhood Adventures
Series

Vincent A. Mastro
illustrations by: Anita Wells

©2014 Vangelo Media

ACA Common Core Critical Thinking Teacher's Manual
Grades 2 - 4
for Aesop's Childhood Adventures Series

Copyright © 2014 by Vincent A. Mastro. All rights reserved.

Except as permitted under the United States Copyright Act, no part of this publication may be reproduced or distributed in any form or by any means, or stored in a database retrieval system, without prior written permission of the publisher.

First published 2014 by *Vangelo Media*
Special discounts are available on quantity purchases. For details, send inquiries to info@vangelomedia.com or visit www.vangelomedia.com.

Printed in the United States of America

Publisher's Cataloging-in-Publication data

Mastro, Vincent.
   ACA common core critical thinking teacher's manual: Grades 2 - 4 for Aesop's childhood adventures / Vincent A. Mastro.
   p. cm.
   ISBN: 978-1-940604-29-9

Audience: educators.
Summary: Pedagogical guidance on applying critical thinking concepts as required by the Common Core standards to the stories of Aesop's Childhood Adventures Series.
Contents: The tortoise and the hare; The goose that laid golden eggs; The boy who cried wolf; and critical thinking worksheets for each story.

1. xxx
2. Aesop's fables—Adaptations. [1. Fables. 2. Folklore.] I. Aesop. II. Title.

Table of Contents

Introduction	**4**
Critical Thinking via Aesop's Fables	**4**
Pedagogic Approach	**6**
The Boy Who Cried Wolf	**8**
Story	9
Guidance	19
Worksheets	20
The Goose that Laid Golden Eggs[1]	**26**
Story	27
Guidance	40
Worksheets	42
The Tortoise and the Hare	**48**
Story	49
Guidance	61
Worksheets	62

---

[1] *The Goose that Laid Golden Eggs* should be used after having worked at least one of the other fables. The 'what if' question for *The Goose that Laid Golden Eggs* results in the same life lesson as opposed to a different life lesson like the other fables. This makes it ideal for contrasting purposes. It also allows the teacher to discuss the concept that different events don't always lead to different results in the same way that different paths or roads can lead to the same destination.

Introduction

This teacher's manual provides pedagogical guidance applying critical thinking concepts to:
- *The Boy Who Cried Wolf*
- *The Goose that Laid Golden Eggs*
- *The Tortoise and the Hare*

The purpose is to facilitate the teacher's efforts to create practical lesson plans. This guidance is provided in the form of tables that describe the critical thinking concept, discussion points, worksheets and the pages of each story.

Spiral bound: The print version of this guide was formatted so that it could be spiral bound. Any printer (such as Kinko's) can do this for a reasonable fee. They will cut the binding, punch the holes and add the spiral binding.

We are always looking for comments, fixes, updates and enhancement. Please contact us at anytime with your suggestions at: info@vangelomedia.com or go to the contact page of our website: www.vangelomedia.com.

Critical Thinking via Aesop's Fables

Critical thinking is the means by which we objectively analyze the pros and cons of a situation in order to make informed decisions. It is a fundamental skill that is of such importance that many colleges and universities require their freshman students to complete an introductory course. The Common Core standard also recognizes the value of critical thinking and has declared it as one of the explicit skills children are to learn. This leaves teachers with the difficult task of teaching this complex skill to elementary school children.

How will children learn critical thinking? The answer is, "it depends."

I am not trivializing the topic; I am however, suggesting children must first understand the concept of "it depends" and how it relates to their daily lives, if they are to think critically.

As we all know, young children are most comfortable with clear rules and "black and white" thinking. The idea that a situation may have multiple answers that depend upon variables and context is a foreign and complex notion to children (and even many adults). Critical thinking begins with the recognition that there are multiple points of view. Each point of view is based on a specific context which, by its very nature, emphasizes one set of characteristics while de-emphasizing the remaining characteristics.

Critical thinking is the evaluation and analysis of the differing points of view for the purpose of determining which point of view is 'more valid'.

Fables are well suited for presenting a situation from at least one point of view. That is because fables are allegorical stories that teach lessons about life. As such, they present a typical problem that children readily understand and can relate too. One or more characters, often animals, resolve the problem thereby presenting the evaluation and analysis from a singular point of view. In this way, fables provide the framework in which the concept of 'it depends' can be introduced to young children. It is as simple as asking a question that causes the child to view the story from another perspective. It is imperative however, that the child fully understands the message of the fable as presented from the original point of view.

Aesop's fables are timeless treasures that have been taught to children for many centuries. They have stood the test of time and are packed with wisdom. 'The Boy Who Cried Wolf' is one of the most well known of Aesop's fables. Children can easily relate to the shepherd boy who is bored and is looking for attention. They can also relate to the unintended consequences of their actions as happened with the shepherd boy who lost a lamb to the wolf because the villagers stopped believing his cries for help.

What if the shepherd boy actually saw the wolf each time he cried for help? What if the wolf was cunning and hid from the villagers? The meaning of the fable changes drastically. It is no longer a fable about the importance of honesty. Instead, it is a fable about the villagers unjustly accusing the shepherd boy of dishonesty. It is a fable about the dangers of jumping to conclusions without knowledge of all the facts.

'What if' questions force an analysis and evaluation from a completely different point of view. Those questions actually create a framework through which the child will begin to think critically. The different perspective is the catalyst for critical thinking and it helps the child realize that 'it depends'.

As you know, there are many adaptations of The Boy Who Cried Wolf. Some simply state that the shepherd boy cried wolf and omit his motives while other versions declare that the boy knowingly lied. The questions above are only appropriate for those versions of the story that do not specifically state that the boy did not see the wolf.

Be prepared for a great discussion as you re-read those sections of the story that open the door to the 'what if' questions. Provoking the children to think critically via 'what if' questions can be applied to any of Aesop's fables. Older children can even be asked to offer their own 'what if' questions. The discussions will be fun and lively. Don't forget to conclude with a discussion on 'it depends'.

Pedagogic Approach

Each fable includes worksheets that ask the following questions:

1. What are the life lessons of Fable X?
2. How would fable X change if ... ?
3. What would the life lesson be if ... ?
4. Are the life lessons the same? Why?

These questions are designed to establish a framework for introducing multiple points of view. The initial point of view is that of the fable as it has been written. That point of view is embodied in the life lesson(s) of the fable. In summary, those life lessons as the means for illustrating different points of view.

The second point of view is introduced in the form of a question "How would fable X change if ... ?". The question requires the child to re-imagine the fable and it should result in significant changes to the original story line. The child is asked what the life lesson(s) would be if the fable was written as suggested by the question. The new life lesson(s) are then compared and contrasted with the life lesson(s) of the original fable.

The 'what if' questions trigger the child to re-imagine the fable; how the characters will respond; and to what degree the events will change. This 're-imagination' mimics what happens with critical thinking by evaluating the situation, without judgement or bias.

The 'what if' questions require the child to evaluate how the events differ between the 2 versions while illustrating how minor changes can have major impacts. This 'what if' technique also provides an opportunity for the child to identify conclusions or assumptions drawn that were not based on facts in the fable. Please note that this often requires prodding from the teacher.

When evaluating any situation, it is important to understand intent and motive. The 5th step in the teacher's guidance/mapping sheet makes motivation and intent the focus of discussion. The purpose is to facilitate the interpretation and analysis of the events and the behaviors of the participants. The purpose of evaluating intent and motive is not to excuse harmful consequences but to understand them within the proper context so that they may be objectively evaluated.

Finally, end the lesson with a discussion of the importance of uncovering all the facts and motivations from all the different points of view. This discussion should include comments about the importance of the unbiased evaluation of the facts and motivations as well. You can do this by discussing the fact that making decisions without critical thinking may lead to erroneous conclusion and therefore bad decisions. The depth of this conversation obviously depends upon the age and sophistication of the students.

Comparative Analysis (optional)

This manual includes these Aesop's fables:
- *The Boy Who Cried Wolf*
- *The Tortoise and the Hare*
- *The Goose that Laid Golden Eggs*

The teacher may compare *The Goose that Laid Golden Eggs* against either of the other two stories because the 'what if' question for *The Goose that Laid Golden Eggs* is very different from the other two fables. The question:

> "How would *The Goose that Laid Golden Eggs* change if the goose stopped laying eggs because the farmer and his wife did not want to spend money to take good care of the goose?"

will result in life lessons that are the same as the original version of the story even though the facts, events and motives are very different. This makes the story ideal for contrasting purposes and it drives home the concept that all events, facts, motives and intentions must be evaluated without preconceived notions or bias. It also allows the teacher to discuss the concept that different events don't always lead to different results.

One way to visually illustrate the concept that different events don't always lead to different results is with a road map. Use a map to show how different paths or roads can lead to the same destination even though the cities and towns that are connected to each path differ.

The Boy Who Cried Wolf

The Boy Who Cried Wolf

"But why Nana, why?" asked Aesop.

With a big smile and a sparkle in her eye, the older one said, "Aesop, I don't know the answer to every question. Sometimes, you have to go and find the answer for yourself."

"I will, Nana. Today is the day I will find out why."

Little Aesop looked up at his grandmother.

He jumped out of her lap and on to the floor. He ran through the den, down the hall and out the door.

It was a beautiful sunny day; perfect weather for Little Aesop to go out and play.

Soon, Little Aesop came to a sloping meadow at the edge of the forest near the village. In the distance he could see a herd of sheep grazing on the sweet grass.

As Aesop continued on his way, he noticed a boy sitting under a tree with a lamb at his feet.

"That boy must be a shepherd," thought Aesop. "I wonder why he looks bored."

Suddenly, the boy stood up.

He had a huge grin on his face. He cupped his hands to his mouth and shouted "**Wolf!**"

Aesop jumped to attention and looked around. He did not see any wolves.

"**Wolf, Wolf!**" yelled the boy.

Aesop looked for the nearest tree and ran toward it. He wanted to be in a safe place.

The boy ran toward the village yelling, "**Wolf, Wolf, Wolf!**"

The villagers came rushing out of their homes carrying pitchforks and guns. They searched the area, but they could not find the wolf.

Aesop could not find any wolves either.

The villagers gathered together and huddled around the shepherd boy. They were talking to him. But, Aesop could not hear what they were saying because he was too far away.

The boy was jumping up and down with excitement. He seemed quite happy. Aesop was confused by this and wondered why the boy did not look frightened.

After a while the villagers walked away and went back to

their homes. They left the shepherd boy to tend the sheep. With a frown on his face, the boy slowly walked back up the hill, toward the flock.

Aesop stayed to watch the shepherd boy because he thought the boy was very funny and quite interesting. The boy did all sorts of odd things like rolling down the hill, running in circles and throwing rocks at trees.

Aesop also noticed that the boy was not doing a good job watching the sheep while he was doing those funny things.

Aesop was about to climb out of the tree and go home when he heard the shepherd boy yell, "**Wolf, Wolf !**"

Again, Aesop jumped to attention and looked around for danger. But he could not find any.

The villagers came rushing out of their homes. They ran

toward the boy. The boy pointed to the forest edge, but there was no wolf. Aesop noticed that the villagers were not happy and they quickly went back to their homes.

Aesop decided to go home, too. As he turned, his eyes opened wide in disbelief. There, across the meadow at the forest edge, was a big, hungry wolf, stalking the flock.

"Oh my!" thought Aesop. "Those poor sheep. What is the boy going to do now?"

"**Wolf, Wolf, Wolf!**" yelled the shepherd boy as loud as he could.

"**Wolf, Wolf, Wolf!**" yelled the frightened shepherd boy as he ran toward the village crying.

But no one was there! None of the villagers came out of their homes.

"**Wolf, Wolf, Wolf!**" he cried, even louder than before.

The villagers, who had been fooled twice, stayed in their warm cozy homes.

The wolf soon caught one of the sheep and took it away.

Aesop was very upset because he wanted the villagers to save the sheep. He ran toward the village where he hid behind a fence.

When the shepherd boy reached the village square he was crying and shaking.

"Where is everyone?" cried the little boy. "The wolf came and took one of the sheep. Why didn't you come out and help me?"

The shepherd boy stood in the middle of the square, all alone. Eventually, the village sage opened her door and said, "A liar will not be believed, even when he speaks the truth."

Little Aesop thought for a moment about what the sage had said. He turned and sadly headed home.

"I'm happy to see you my little one," said Aesop's grandmother, who was sitting in the den. "Did you find what you were looking for? Did you get the answer to your questions?"

"No," said Aesop as he climbed into his grandmother's lap, "I still do not know why. But I do know that no one will believe a liar even when he speaks the truth."

"That is right, Aesop. Tell me more."

"Well, I went to the meadow by the forest's edge where I saw a shepherd boy tending sheep …"

When Aesop was finished telling his grandmother everything that happened, she looked at the young one with a big smile and a sparkle in her eye and said, "It sounds like you had a great adventure. I know you did not find what you were looking for, but you did learn the importance of always telling the truth."

She then hugged Aesop and said, "Don't worry about your questions, Aesop. Eventually, you will find the answers to all of them because you have perseverance."

The Boy Who Cried Wolf

Critical Thinking

[1] What are the life lessons of *The Boy Who Cried Wolf*?
- A liar will not be believed even when he speaks the truth.
- Unintended consequences happen.
- Honesty is the best policy.

[2] How would *The Boy Who Cried Wolf* change if the shepherd boy actually saw the wolf each time he cried for help? What if the villagers did not see the wolf because he was cunning and hid each time the shepherd boy called for help?

There are two possible outcomes. Either the hare would have won the race after waking up from his nap or no one would have won because both of them were no longer on the track.

[3] What would the life lesson be if the shepherd boy actually saw the wolf each time he cried for help? What if the villagers did not see the wolf because he was cunning and hid each time the shepherd boy called for help?
- You **must be** the fastest or best to win so don't bother to try if you are not.
- People don't like it when others boast.
- Bragging can hurt people.

[4] Are the life lessons the same? Why?

These are the same:
- People don't like it when others boast.
- Bragging can hurt people.

This life lesson:
- You don't have to be the fastest or best to win.

Is changed to:
- You **must be** the fastest or best to win so don't bother to try if you are not.

because that is the reasoning most likely used by the tortoise to rationalize her decision to quit.

This life lesson is deleted because the toroise gave up:
- Anything is possible with perseverance.

[5] Discussion points.

The purpose of this lesson is to introduce the idea that a situation may have multiple outcomes depending upon the facts, the events that occurred (or did not occur), the actions of the participants, the participant's interpretation of the facts and their motivations. Items #1 - 4 above force the child to recognize that the story changes and some of the life lessons also change as a result of a change in the facts.

The final step is to introduce the the concept of motivations. Re-introduce item #2 above and emphasize the idea that Tortoise was demoralized by the speed of the hare. Then ask How would the story change if the tortoise gave up because she got injured and could not run anymore? This changes the tortoise's motivations for giving up and therefore the first life lesson of #3 above is no longer true.

End with a discussion of the importance of uncovering all the facts and motivations from all the different points of view otherwise you may come to an erroneous conclusion and therefore make a bad decision.

Critical Thinking Worksheets

for

The Boy Who Cried Wolf

What are the life lessons of *The Boy Who Cried Wolf?*

Name: _____ Date: _____

How would *The Boy Who Cried Wolf* change if the shepherd boy actually saw the wolf each time he cried for help? What if the villagers did not see the wolf because he was cunning and hid each time the shepherd boy called for help?

What would the life lesson be if the shepherd boy actually saw the wolf each time he cried for help? What if the villagers did not see the wolf because he was cunning and hid each time the shepherd boy called for help?

Are the life lessons the same? Why?

The Goose that Laid Golden Eggs

The Goose that Laid Golden Eggs

"But why Nana, why?" asked Aesop.

With a big smile and a sparkle in her eye, the older one said, "Aesop, I don't know the answer to every question. Sometimes, you have to go and find the answer for yourself."

"I will, Nana. Today is the day I will find out why."

Little Aesop looked up at his grandmother.

He jumped out of her lap and on to the floor. He ran through the den, down the hall and out the door.

It was a beautiful sunny day; perfect weather for Little Aesop to go out and play.

Soon, Little Aesop came upon a man sitting under a tree. It looked like the man had been crying. Aesop did not want to disturb the man so he hid behind a rock.

"Hi Aesop," said a familiar voice from somewhere nearby.

"Is that you, Owl? Where are you?"

"Yes, it is me. I am up here in the tree. Come sit with me."

Aesop carefully snuck up the tree to a branch near the owl.

"Do you know why that man is sad?" asked Aesop.

"Well, yes," said the owl. "He is sad because he was greedy."

Aesop was confused because greedy and sad are two different things. "I don't understand," said Aesop. "He looks sad to me."

"Well," said the owl "this man is a farmer who had a goose that laid eggs of gold.

When he saw the first golden egg he thought the goose was sick or maybe someone was playing a trick on him. He could not believe that the goose had laid an egg that was made of real gold.

"Why?" asked Aesop.

"Well," said the owl, "geese don't lay eggs of gold, do they?"

Aesop thought for a moment and agreed, geese do not lay eggs of gold.

The owl continued the story…

"The first thing the farmer did the next day was check to see if the goose had laid another golden egg. To his surprise, the egg was there, sitting in the nest, glistening.

The farmer took the egg from the nest and put it in his pants pocket. He grabbed his coat, left the house and headed straight to town. He walked into the jewelry store and showed the jeweler the two golden eggs. The jeweler was very surprised by the two eggs and bought them for lots of money.

The farmer was very happy, and very thankful.

Aesop looked at the owl with big round eyes and said, "I would be happy and thankful too."

The next morning the farmer got up early to see if the goose had laid another golden egg. Sure enough, the nest had another egg of gold.

The farmer took the egg, put it in his pocket and grabbed his coat. He walked as fast as he could to the jewelry store where the jeweler bought the egg for lots of money.

The farmer was very happy and headed home. As he walked through town he saw many wonderful things in the shops. He bought all that he could, including a wheel barrow to carry it all.

When the man got home, he showed his wife all of the things that he had bought. There were things they needed very badly, and there were things they really did not need at all.

The wife was very happy and very excited. She told her husband that she wanted to take good care of their magical goose.

She wanted to buy it a comfy nest and the best, tastiest goose food she could find. All she needed was for the goose to lay another golden egg.

"Why did she need another golden egg?" asked Aesop.

"Well," replied Owl, "so that they had enough money to buy all of those things for the goose."

"The next morning the farmer and his wife got up early to see if there was another golden egg. Sure enough, there it was. They hid the egg in a safe place and started their daily chores.

The next morning …"

"Wait!" said Aesop. "Didn't they go to town to buy food and a comfy nest for the goose?"

"Well, no," said the owl, "they thought it was too long a walk for just one egg. They waited two whole weeks before the farmer finally went into town. By then, he had a dozen golden eggs.

The jeweler bought each and every one of the 12 eggs from the farmer. The farmer now had more money than he had ever seen in his life.

The farmer could not believe his good fortune. He visited every store in town and bought all sorts of things for himself, his wife, and the house. But, he did not buy anything for the goose."

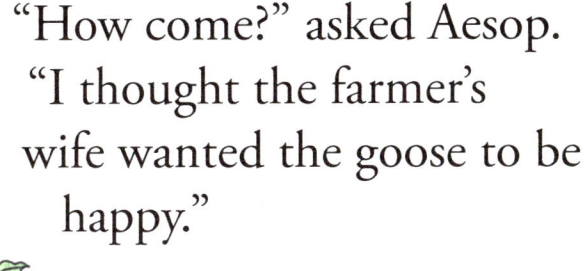

"How come?" asked Aesop. "I thought the farmer's wife wanted the goose to be happy."

"Well, the farmer had become greedy," said the owl.

"I don't understand," said Aesop.

"Well, the farmer decided that the goose did not need a comfy nest or good food. He had a plan. He was going to take all of the goose's eggs without having to wait for her to lay them."

Aesop was puzzled, "How was he going to do that?"

"Well," said the owl, "the farmer killed the goose thinking he could get all the eggs that were inside her."

"Oh no!" gasped Aesop. "What a horrible thing to do."

"Well, yes Aesop, it was a terrible thing to do."

"How many eggs did he get?" asked Aesop.

"Well, none! Not a single one!" said the owl. "The farmer realized that he should not have killed the goose. He should have waited for the goose to lay the eggs instead of being so greedy."

"Is that why he is sad?" asked Aesop.

"Well, yes," said the owl.

"You are right, Owl," agreed Aesop. "The farmer is greedy and he should be sad. He did a terrible thing and I feel sad for the goose. Now I understand how someone can be both sad and greedy. Thank you for telling me the story."

"You are welcome Aesop."

Aesop smiled at Owl and said 'Bye. I have to get home now; my Nana is waiting for me."

Aesop then climbed down from the tree and headed home.

"I'm happy to see you my little one," said Aesop's grandmother who was sitting in the den.

"Did you find what you were looking for? Did you get the answer to your questions?"

"No," said Aesop as he climbed into his grandmother's lap, "I still do not know why. But I do know that people sometimes do bad things when they are greedy."

"That is right, Aesop. Tell me more."

"Well, I met Owl today, and he told me about a farmer that was both greedy and sad …"

When Aesop was finished telling his

grandmother everything that happened, she looked at the young one with a big smile and a sparkle in her eye and said, "It sounds like you had a great adventure. I know you did not find what you were looking for, but you did learn that greed will often lead to a bad deed."

She then hugged Aesop and said, "Don't worry about your questions, Aesop. Eventually, you will find the answers to all of them because you have perseverance".

The Goose that Laid Golden Eggs

Critical Thinking

The Goose that Laid Golden Eggs should be used after having worked at least one of the other fables. The 'what if' question for this fable results in the same life lesson as opposed to a different life lesson like the other fables. This makes it ideal for contrasting purposes i.e. it is the counter-example. It also allows the teacher to discuss the concept that different events don't always lead to different results in the same way that different paths or roads can lead to the same destination.

[1] What are the life lessons of *The Goose that Laid Golden Eggs*?   • Greed often motivates people to do bad things.   • A person can exhibit multiple emotions at the same time i.e. greed and sadness.
[2] How would *The Goose that Laid Golden Eggs* change if the goose stopped laying eggs because the farmer and his wife did not want to spend money to take good care of the goose?   The goose would not have died but would have become sick enough to stop egg production. The farmer would still be sad that he allowed the goose to become ill. The decision to not spend money on good food etc for the goose was an act of greed via neglect.
[3] What would the life lesson be if the farmer did not kill the goose but the goose stopped laying eggs of any kind because he and his wife did not want to spend money to take good care of the goose?   • Greed often motivates people to do bad things.   • A person can exhibit multiple emotions at the same time i.e. greed and sadness.
[4] Are the life lessons the same? Why?   Yes, the life lessons would be the same because greed was the motivation for not taking care of the goose... "… because the farmer and his wife did not want to spend money to take good care of the goose?".   One could argue that the farmer did not kill the goose therefore did not do an explicit act of greed. This would be a good opportunity to discuss the notion that it is often valuable to identify what is missing or what did not happen when evaluating a situation.
[5] Discussion points.   The purpose of this lesson is to provide a contrast to the lessons presented in the other two fables. This lesson illustrates the fact that changes in the events and facts of a story do not always result in a different outcome. In contrast, the other two lessons in this manual illustrate the idea that a situation may have multiple outcomes depending upon the facts; the events that occurred (or did not occur); the actions of the participants; the participant's interpretation of the facts; and their motivations.   The 'what if' question includes motivation i.e. "… because the farmer and his wife did not want to spend money to take good care of the goose?" this is important because their motive was greed and they purposefully did not take care of the goose, allowing its health to decline.   End with a discussion of the importance of uncovering all the facts and motivations from all the different points of view and caution the children that different facts, different events, even different motives do not necessarily result in different outcomes

Critical Thinking Worksheets

for

The Goose that Laid Golden Eggs

What are the life lessons of *The Goose that Laid Golden Eggs?*

Name: _____ Date: _____

How would *The Goose that Laid Golden Eggs* change if the goose stopped laying eggs because the farmer and his wife did not want to spend money to take good care of the goose?

What would the life lesson be if the goose stopped laying eggs because the farmer and his wife did not want to spend money to take good care of the goose?

Are the life lessons the same? Why?

Name: _____ **Date:** _____

The Tortoise and the Hare

The Tortoise and the Hare

"But why Nana, why?" asked Aesop.

With a big smile and a sparkle in her eye, the older one said, "Aesop, I don't know the answer to every question. Sometimes, you have to go and find the answer for yourself."

"I will, Nana. Today is the day I will find out why."

Little Aesop looked up at his grandmother. He jumped

out of her lap and on to the floor. He ran through the den, down the hall and out the door.

It was a beautiful sunny day, perfect weather for Little Aesop to go out and play.

Soon, Little Aesop came upon his friends the fox, the hare, the two mice, and the tortoise.

"Hi everyone," said Aesop.

The hare turned to Aesop and said, "I was just saying that I can run so fast that I can beat anyone in a race."

The tortoise shook her head sadly and asked, "Why do you need to brag so much?"

"It is not bragging when it is true," said the hare.

The other animals looked at each other and said nothing.

The hare turned toward the tortoise and laughed at her. "Look how short your legs are. You must be the slowest of us all!"

Aesop was disappointed in the hare for being so rude.

The tortoise replied, "I may be slow and have short legs, but I have something that you do not have."

The hare chuckled and said, "That is right, Tortoise. You do have something that none of us have. You have a big heavy shell to slow you down."

"There you go boasting again," said the tortoise.

"Do you think you can beat me in a race?"

The hare burst into laughter, as did all the other animals, except for Aesop. Aesop was worried that the tortoise would lose the race. He did not want her to be sad and he knew the hare would never stop bragging if he won.

"Is that a joke?" asked the hare. "I could dance the whole way and still beat someone as slow as you."

The mouse jumped up and down with excitement and yelled, "A race, a race! I'm going to get my checkered flag."

When the mouse returned he stood by the tree and said, "The race will start here. You will run past the big boulder, and go down the hill. Then you will run around the clover field and back up the hill to this tree. The first one to the finish line wins the race."

The tortoise was ready at the starting line, while the hare was gibbering and jabbering with all the other animals.

Aesop was worried that the race was much too long for the tortoise. He did not want her to lose.

"On your mark … get set … GO!" yelled the mouse.

The tortoise pushed herself forward, taking one slow step at a time. She was moving as fast as her little legs could

take her, but she did not get very far. All the other animals pointed at her and laughed, except for Aesop.

The hare was laughing too. They laughed until their bellies ached.

The mouse saw that the hare had not yet started the race so he yelled, "Go hare, go!"

Swoosh!

The hare took off like a dart. He ran past the tortoise, by the boulder, then down the hill, and was out of sight.

The tortoise had not gone very far at all. She had not even reached the big boulder. One of the animals yelled, "You should just give up, Tortoise. There is no way you are going to win. You are much too slow."

Aesop called out to the tortoise, "Go, Tortoise, go! You can do it!"

The tortoise looked over and smiled at Aesop and said, "I will never give up. I have something that the hare does not have." But no one understood what the tortoise was talking about.

Aesop and all the other animals ran to the top of the hill to see how far the hare had gone. To everyone's surprise, the hare was lying down next to a stump playing with the clover.

The hare saw the animals and yelled, "Look at all this clover. I am going to find one with four leaves."

After a while, the hare got bored looking for a four leaf clover and he fell asleep.

Aesop could not believe that the hare had fallen asleep during the middle of a race. It was at that moment, that Aesop understood what the tortoise meant when she had said, that she had something that the hare did not have.

Aesop smiled and walked to the finish line because he now knew, the tortoise would win the race.

Meanwhile, the tortoise just plodded on, taking one slow step at a time, focusing only on the finish line. Eventually, the tortoise passed the sleeping hare, who was snoring as he napped in the clover. She continued slowly on her way.

When the hare woke up from his nap, he saw that the tortoise was just about to cross the finish line. He leapt up, and ran as fast as he could.

But he was too late. The tortoise had crossed the finish line first and won the race!

"Congratulations!" said the fox. "It looks like slow and steady wins the race."

"That is right," replied the tortoise. "I have perseverance."

"What is perseverance?" asked the fox.

Aesop knew that the tortoise won the race because she had focused only on the race and did not give up.

Little Aesop could not wait to go home and tell his Nana about perseverance. He said good bye to his friends and headed home.

"I'm happy to see you my little one," said Aesop's grandmother, who was sitting in the den. "Did you find what you were looking for? Did you get the answer to your questions?"

"No," said Aesop as he climbed into his grandmother's lap, "I still do not know why, but I did learn that slow and steady can win a race, and I don't like it when people boast."

"That is very good Aesop, tell me more."

"Well, I saw a race today, Nana, where the tortoise beat the hare…"

When Aesop was finished telling his grandmother everything that happened, she looked at the young one with a big smile and a sparkle in her eye and said, "It sounds like you had a great adventure today. I know you did not find what you were looking for, but you did learn that bragging can hurt people and anything is possible with perseverance."

She then hugged Aesop and said, "Don't worry about your questions, Aesop. Eventually, you will find the answers to all of them because you have perseverance too."

The Tortoise and the Hare

[1] What are the life lessons of *The Tortoise and the Hare*?

- You don't have to be the fastest or best to win.
- Anything is possible with perseverance.
- People don't like it when others boast.
- Bragging can hurt people.

[2] How would *The Tortoise and the Hare* change if the tortoise gave up after the hare ran past her?

There are two possible outcomes. Either the hare would have won the race after waking up from his nap or no one would have won because both of them were no longer on the track.

[3] What would the life lesson be if the tortoise gave up after the hare ran past her?

- You **must be** the fastest or best to win so don't bother to try if you are not.
- People don't like it when others boast.
- Bragging can hurt people.

[4] Are the life lessons the same? Why?

These are the same:
- People don't like it when others boast.
- Bragging can hurt people.

This life lesson:
- You don't have to be the fastest or best to win.

Is changed to:
- You **must be** the fastest or best to win so don't bother to try if you are not.

because that is the reasoning most likely used by the tortoise to rationalize her decision to quit.

This life lesson is deleted because the toroise gave up:
- Anything is possible with perseverance.

[5] Discussion points.

The purpose of this lesson is to introduce the idea that a situation may have multiple outcomes depending upon the facts, the events that occurred (or did not occur), the actions of the participants, the participant's interpretation of the facts and their motivations. Items #1 - 4 above force the child to recognize that the story changes and some of the life lessons also change as a result of a change in the facts.

The final step is to introduce the the concept of motivations. Re-introduce item #2 above and emphasize the idea that Tortoise was demoralized by the speed of the hare. Then ask **How would the story change if the tortoise gave up because she got injured and could not run anymore?** This changes the tortoise's motivations for giving up and therefore the first life lesson of #3 above is no longer true.

End with a discussion of the importance of uncovering all the facts and motivations from all the different points of view otherwise you may come to an erroneous conclusion and therefore make a bad decision.

Critical Thinking Worksheets

for

The Tortoise and the Hare

What are the life lessons of *The Tortoise and the Hare*?

Name: _____ **Date:** _____

How would *The Tortoise and the Hare* change if the tortoise gave up after the hare ran past her?

Name: _____ **Date:** _____

What would the life lesson be if the tortoise gave up after the hare ran past her?

Are the life lessons the same? Why?

Name: _____ Date: _____